The Most Beautiful Woman in the Room

Chapter 1 (OBSERVATION)

- *The setting*
- *Listen with your eyes*
- *Contact*
- *The Conversation*

Chapter 2 (THE PROCESS)

- *The process*
- *The compliment*
- *The close*
- *The compliment (2)*

Chapter 3 (Questions, Questions, Questions)

- *How reliable are you*
- *How dependable are you*
- *How much do you cost*
- *How much service do you provide*
- *Are you easy to use*

Chapter 4 (MAINTENANCE)

- *Personal Discovery*
- *Walking through the door*
- *Do nothing for free*
- *At the end of the day*

This book is dedicated to the 6 women that have influenced my life the most: Grandmothers: Elizabeth & Mary, Mothers: Charlotte & Deborah, Daughter: Victoria, Life Partner, Best Friend, and Future Wife: Michelle B.

PREFACE

There is nothing original. The biblical character, King Solomon, known as the wisest man who has ever lived said, "There is nothing new under the sun," so I accept this to be true. Every word in this book has been written by someone else at some point and time. I only offer you a different perspective on the same information. If I can influence just one person to see something different that will help them change their internal perspective on not just obtaining their dream but LIFE, then this was worth the effort. For example, there are millions of people that lose large amounts of weight every year. At one time, these individuals were viewed as people with a weight problem and may have been called, "fat people." However, through a conscious effort on their part, a methodical & systematic plan, and a deliberate course of action, they are now in shape. The question or perspective is not "did they lose weight?" The question is, did they simply change the way that we viewed them? One may argue that these people never changed at all, merely, they changed the way that we perceive them. Maybe, they always were thin and the public just viewed them as overweight. I realize that this is a bit far- fetched but guess what? Many things that we now believe in were once far-fetched. Who could imagine just 50 years ago that we would be walking around talking on a device that has no wires to anyone in the world? Or better yet, paying $1.09 for bottled water. Yet here we are. My goal with this book is to simply get the reader to be open to a new perspective and realize that anything you want in life can be obtained through conscious, deliberate, methodical actions.

CHAPTER 1

The Setting

Here I am again. I am standing in front of a new group of people who have come to be trained, coached, or mentored in the fine art of sales. Interestingly, what they are really stating is that they desperately want to change the outcome of their lives by taking control of it. Sales is a volatile career path that only pays dividends to the bold and the courageous. The individuals who are willing to face and defeat the person in the mirror, typically get paid the most. My job is to put you at ease and let you know that it can be taught, learned and applied with great ease. No matter what your background, personality, career or gender… Great sales people are made, not born. With anything involving success, one must constantly, tirelessly, and emphatically work on your skills regardless of your talent level. The best students are the humblest who have eagerly checked their ego at the door and have the ability to view the similarities of a situation instead of looking at the differences. Ok, so let's go. Most people that are in the sales field (which, in my opinion, includes every person on this earth since we are always selling something!) are always looking for what they can say to get someone to buy something from them. A person new to sales may be looking for some detailed phrase that will somehow magically get the customer to purchase their particular product/service. The professional may be looking for information on the principle of how to apply specific phrases or words. Seasoned or beginner, the end result is that we all are looking for more predictability and higher closing ratios. This is where the challenge begins since there are an infinite amount of outcomes to even the simplest question. It would be a good idea to widen our gaze a bit. Maybe look at this from a macro level and gain some insight on a concept that will fluidly apply itself to the infinite. Most would be surprised at how simple it really is. So we are going to stop with all the guru talk and have some fun.

I believe in having a very interactive class where people can ask questions and not just hear some dude up front, talking. No need to feed my ego. So the class usually starts off asking me the same old questions like… "How do you do …?" "What is the right way to do….?" and then my favorite question of all "How do you close, what is the proper way to close…?" Although these are all good questions, and seemingly the most urgent, it really is not a good place to start. It is kind of like giving you the answer to a math problem without understanding how you got it. Yet, this is the reason why many people come and get trained so they can CLOSE A DEAL. Let me state this for the record: Closing is an art form and, with proper execution, will be like beautiful music being conducted where the woodwinds, brass, strings & percussion are all playing harmoniously together. Unfortunately, most do not understand this and, thus, little to no music is created at all. Why is closing so important you may ask? To be honest, it is the measuring stick to our "perceived success" (mental realness), made manifest or tangible (physical realness), a reward for doing a good job. The obstacle in the way of your success is one word…FEAR!

F-False E-Evidence A-Appearing R-Real

Many of us have heard this before, however, what makes this so crazy is that the entire process is taking place inside your mind. The process is about future events THAT MAY NOT EVEN HAPPEN! It gets better! Inside of this mental environment are also some records of past events that did not turn out so well. So when a person is trying to move forward, they have the weight of the past on their shoulders while dodging imaginary obstacles that they have conjured completely out of thin air about events that probably will not happen. Sounds ridiculous but this is the process that we all go through when we live a fear based life. This is what, we as people, are dealing with and with a bit of courage we can take advantage of it!

In my dealings, I have found that one of the best ways to gain a wider level of understanding is to relate an abstract thought or process with something more familiar. I have chosen my process "The Most Beautiful Woman in the Room" approach. Conceptually, most have fallen prey to someone's beauty where it seemed to almost cause paralysis. The mere thought of going up to this person cause instantaneous fear and all of the effects that go along with it. Ironically, this is the same EXACT feeling people get when thinking about how to attack their greatest dreams and most intense desires. As you learn how to methodically talk to "The Most Beautiful Woman in the Room" you will also learn how to close that "BIG DEAL". Let me state this now so you do not miss it… **Life, Sales,**

"The Woman"… they are all the same. So learning how to successfully procure one of these is successful procurement of all. Remember, this is not just any woman, but the most beautiful woman you have every laid eyes on. The kind of woman that when you first see her, your breath becomes short, your heart begins to race with the anticipation of love, and you begin to perspire at the mere thought of that first real interaction. The smell of her perfume sends you into a trance, and you can't get her out of our head! THAT WOMAN. What are you going to do? Are you going to look at her all night (that's a bit weird) or are you going to find a way to get what you want? (**Remember…Life, Sales, the Woman… all the same**). Now that I have your attention, it is time to make a statement. **There are very few things in the life, if any, that you can't obtain but you must be willing to lose your ego in order to win the prize.** Life is a series of processes and stages. Sales is a series of processes and stages. Talking to the woman is a (you guessed it) series of processes and stages. Understand the processes, complete the stages, and win the game!

I make a lot of statements in order to create a foundation that we can build on. It is necessary that we simply accept them, by the way, they will be in bold.

A sell is a sell. It does not matter what the product or service is… at the end of the day, a sell is a sell. You must remove your emotion to think clearly on this (easier said than done). Most people actually think that you need to know every single little detail of what they represent in order to sell. NOT TRUE. Some famous person said "The devil is in the details" so where in the world did people get that detailed knowledge is the key to closing a deal? That would be similar to knowing all the different ways to paint your house but simply knowing does not paint the house. Actions paint the house. It gets better. Detailed knowledge is like painting the house with a small, fine paint brush. How long is that going to take? In school, people were taught how to be smart, not great! There are so many examples in history of great men who barely made it out of high school, employing people with detailed knowledge (I hope you got that).

An example of an organization who does very well without having a lot of detailed information about what they offer would be The Girl Scouts of America. This is genius! I mean they really have this down to a complete science. The cookie manufacturer found a way to get little girls to sell their cookies by employing them for a "good cause" (which automatically employs the parents). The girls go and sell the cookies door to door or through the efforts of the parents to make sure they receive a prize. Question? How much information does the average Girl Scout know about the cookies? Probably as much as is printed on the paper and that's it. All she gives you is the purpose of why they are doing it, the kind of cookies they have, and how many do you want to purchase. Pretty simple. Any additional information you can look up yourself. They have millions of orders every single year. Why? Is it the best cookie you ever tasted? Does it have the best ingredients? Is it even convenient? Most people forget they even bought the boxes because it takes so long to get it! **PEOPLE BUY FROM PEOPLE TO SUPPORT A CAUSE OR A NEED.** So why do so many people have a challenge with this process? People are too busy trying to be smart instead of being great.

Great people typically do not have all the answers so they surround themselves with Smart people to find them! Smart people manage what Great people lead. Great people trust the process, smart people trust themselves.

I am going somewhere with this so just bear with me a bit... I am about to bring it home.

A process can also be viewed as a circle of events. If you walk in a circle you will eventually come back to where you started. If you walk in the process enough times, the process becomes predictable. Conversely, smart people use information as their ultimate source of power. Since information is always changing and what may be true today may not be true tomorrow, so does the person depending on the source. Therefore, a process never changes and is trustworthy. Information is always changing and is not!

The algebraic equation: $x + y = z$

was created to predict an outcome with a fair amount of certainty. This equation works because:

x= variables (Things that change, information, perspective)
y=constants (Things that do not change, processes)
z= predictability.

A true salesperson should be able to sell ANYTHING, at any given moment, at any given time, to anyone in need of the product or service. It is not because they know everything, but because they follow a process that never changes and apply it to situations which always change. That is a key statement. To further qualify the above statement in an effort to be accurate, please focus on the part that says "ANYONE IN NEED!" The job of the sales person is not to tell a person all about the product or service. Their job is to **DISCOVER THE NEED AND MAKE THEM WANT IT, BECAUSE IT POSSIBLY MAY BE THE SOLUTION TO THEIR PROBLEM!**

Why in the world would I say that… well, let me put it to you this way… people buy what they want but pray and beg for what they need. Most sales people are so busy trying to learn the product that they forget to learn the process.

The amateur sales person will begin something like this…. "I have this product"… "It is round, has pretty colors, and feels good, will you buy this?" I suggest a different approach. This approach is, "The Most Beautiful Woman in the Room" approach.

Ok, in order to convey this process we are going to have to take you to the average setting to paint the correct picture. Hopefully, you will see the application.

Say you are at a local bar & grill with 10 of your co-workers for an evening of relaxation and conversation. The night is young and you are glad that work is over. You become engaged in an amazing conversation about something that happened earlier in the day with one of your buddies. As you turn, someone catches your eye. Wow, the most attractive woman you have ever seen just walked in and is standing 20 feet in front of you. This woman was literally constructed out of the vast deposits of your mind's deepest and most vast dreams of what a perfect 10 would be. As she seems to float around the room you realize that this stunning vision of perfection has all the outward qualities anyone could ever ask for. You are almost paralyzed with her beauty. She is attracting attention from everyone! Immediately, your mind begins to race with thoughts of you and her. Every time you look at her you get butterflies. As you watch her for the next hour or so, you notice that every guy that walks up to her is getting gunned down almost immediately. Even the guy who has the "six pack abs" good looks and dashing smile had no chance. As you watch this scenario a few times over the night, your dreams of you having a chance with her are slowly turning to doubt. Your initial thoughts of bliss are being replaced with all the things you do not have to attract such a beautiful specimen. However, if you have any backbone at all, your ego will not let you leave without at least trying. So you begin to think, "Let me work my way up to this person" and begin to mingle with people who you THINK you have a chance with, as a bit of a warm up. Now you are working the room, keeping an eye on her hoping that this vixen notices you and gives you some kind of starting ground to begin a conversation. Finally, you can't stand it any longer and work up enough nerve and begin the approach. You walk up and SAY "Hi, my name is" or "What is your name?" "Do you live around here?" "What brings you out this evening?" What happens next? Rat-a-tat-tat… You just got gunned down. You feel 2 inches high and all your buddies are laughing at you. As the night moves on, the woman becomes more and more irritated and finally, packs up and leaves. What happened? Why did she leave? More importantly, why did she not leave with you?

What is interesting about this particular situation is that people tend to get the same feeling when they are thinking about their dreams. More specifically, sales people get this feeling when they think or see a big possible client. You will hear them say "Wow… how would you like to do business with them…" What's the problem? The problem is … the right questions were not asked. Yes, it's that simple. It is all about the questions. Let me quickly help you understand… **Your physical beauty has little to no value if you have no mental beauty! Your mental beauty is based upon how interesting you become. Your level of being interesting is based on the quality of your questions and your ability to accurately communicate them.** You see, The Most Beautiful Woman in the Room is just like that major firm that you have yet to sell your product or service to. Every single sales person that goes after the firm gets denied because of the same old approach… "I have the best product… it will save you money…we can beat anyone's price!!!" Did you ask what was important to them? **Most people don't ask, they assume.** Beautiful women experience the same come on line every single time they go anywhere. I am sure that the outcomes are usually the same. What you may not realize is that, The Most Beautiful Woman in the Room, is usually the loneliest person in the room and they are just waiting for that one person to connect with! Sure they are surrounded by people, but have not connected with any of them. Just like that one client you can't seem to sell your product to. Again, I suggest a different approach.

Listen with your eyes

Before we get into the actual approach, there are a few things that you must become aware of when dealing with what you want. Albert Einstein said *"No problem can be solved from the same level of consciousness that created it."* Simply put, once you are aware of the problem, you must become even more aware to understand the solution. This is a good time to introduce what I believe most people take too seriously. Setting plays a very important role when it comes to people. **Setting is to sales, what soil is to seeds**. Inside the seed is the blueprint for a beautiful tree, if only it is placed in the correct soil. A person may be perfect for what you have but are they open to receive it? For example, if the perfect client is sitting in church, this probably is not the right time to talk to him about how your product can enhance their business. Becoming more masterful in sales has a lot to do with becoming more keenly aware of the particular environment or setting that is before you. Let's apply this back to the beautiful woman to see how it may apply because remember... Life, Sales, or The Most Beautiful Woman in the Room... all the same thing!

The woman of your dreams walks into an after work establishment at 5:30pm. Your first assumption may be that she is there to relax. This is a pretty good guess, however, there is an infinite amount of other possibilities that you must be open to. To master life, sales, or the woman, it would be wise to remain open to all possibilities and not so bent to just one answer. The woman may be there to meet some clients from out of town, or there to discuss some very important details of clients with her co-workers. You never know. You must be aware of that. If you are listening with your eyes, yes, I said listening with your eyes; she may leave you some clues.

By the way, every major client you will ever deal with will tell you the same thing if you just listen with your eyes. If you happen to get an appointment with one of these magical clients and walk into their office, just look around at the setting and see what it is telling you. You may see pictures of family on the desk, or trophies on the mantle, or even a desk that is covered in papers. Each one of these scenarios is telling you about the person before they even open their mouth. They are telling you what is really important to them. Pictures of family usually suggest that they are a person who puts their family first. This person may think that the firm that they represent is also their family, thus, the direction of the firm is more important than their personal opinion. They will protect the firm at all cost. A seasoned sales person sees this immediately and will present their material in like fashion. Trophies may suggest that they are very competitive and want to be recognized for their efforts so present your material with this in mind. A desk full of papers to some might mean that they are unorganized, however, it also might mean that they are extremely busy, understaffed, and they are wearing many hats at once. A seasoned sales person may suggest how their particular product/service may help them save time by creating simple organizational processes, thereby, saving them money. All this information is being presented to you before you even say one word. Setting applies to not just one's physical environment but also mental. What a person habitually thinks about creates a mental environment that they carry with them where ever they go. In order to listen to this, one must patiently MENTALLY see what is going on inside of their mind by asking the right questions. This process involves creating the correct circumstances that would allow the other person to begin communication with you. The Most Beautiful Woman in the Room is saying the same thing so before you take that shot of tequila, just watch for a moment and see what she is saying. I promise that if you are listening with your eyes, you will hear what she is telling you. Gathering this type of information before you approach anyone will put you ahead for 90% of the competition. Also, if you find yourself in the unique position to find out information before-hand, like on the internet, it may help you set yourself apart from the rest. The information that you are looking for is "what makes this person unique." Now, what do you do with this new found information?

Contact (say nothing but do all the talking)

So, you think you know what to say now. MISTAKE. You should be more clueless than when you first started! This is good. If you have that feeling that means that you are now open to go in any direction that the conversation may lead you but WHAT DO YOU SAY?! Before I get to what you say, let me tell you what you really have with respect to an opportunity. You got about 90 seconds. That's it! Most people can and will make their decision about you that fast. The challenge in the entire scenario is "How can I buy myself another 90 seconds?" The longer the conversation, the more likely it will be that you will find what you are looking for! By the way, you are looking for one thing and one thing only, MORE OPPORTUNITY! Let's apply this to the woman and an average guy's conversation.

Biff (an average guy) walks up to this The Most Beautiful Woman in the Room. In Biff's mind he feels that he has the best chance because he works out 6 times a week, has perfect teeth, speaks well, drives a nice car, have a great job, dress very nicely…

(I think you get the picture). He sits down and says… "Hi, what's your name?" Not a bad intro, could be better, but let's go with it. As the woman proceeds to tell Biff her name, he then replies with "My name if Biff". Biff now says "So… what do you do for a living?" It's a bit intrusive but not out of line. She says, "Well, I work for ABC company as the Senior Branch manager over operation"… Here comes the first mistake… Biff then replies with "Well I work for XYZ attorney firm and am a partner in the company." He then begins this monologue about his resume and what his job entails…

blah…blah…blah. At the end of his story, he says "Here is my business card, let's get together for lunch sometime." She takes it and puts it in her purse along with 90 other ones. As he walks away, he is feeling pretty good because he got her business card and plans to call her later on. Biff has got about a 20% chance of ever seeing her again.

There is a secret at this stage that very few people are consciously aware of. This secret is so obvious that we miss it. The secret is really a question which you can seldom go wrong with. The secret is… **How do you get the person to talk about themselves?** That's it. I could stop writing right now and walk away and most would have more success than before reading this book. Getting this beautiful woman to talk about herself is the key to gaining more opportunity with her. Likewise, if you are sitting in front of the CEO of XYZ Company who last year was the industry leader in widgets, ask them why they were so successful. It really isn't a bad place to start because most are proud of what they have done and may give you an indication of what makes them special. It could be a new relationship with a client or maybe a different process than their competitors. The purpose of the question is twofold. First, it provides you great information without leading the conversation. If you listen closely, they may tell you what is really important to them. Secondly, it shows that you are really interested in them and their SUCCESSFUL process. Remember, you are looking for what makes them unique! You will get great information that could possibly help you with your presentation later in the conversation. The worst thing that could happen is that you bought yourself another 90 seconds. This is only the beginning. The kinds of questions that need to be asked at this stage of the game are all open ended questions. An open ended question is defined as a question that cannot be answered by a yes or no. To qualify this further, the question should be structured so that the person that you are asking it to… literally has to think about the answer. There is a pretty good indication that you may have asked the right question to the person if they stop or pause in the conversation, and look up to the left. You might be saying "WHAT?" looking up to the left? YES, when a person is asked a question that requires some conscious thought, then they are accessing the creative part of the brain, therefore, they look up to the left. (This is a decent rule of thumb that you can have some fun with). Quite simple if you think about it. Try it on yourself and see. You will notice that when looking up to the left you are usually in deep thought, searching for an answer or solution. By the way, looking up to the right has meaning as well. This is the part of the brain where facts are placed. So, if you see a person who is looking up to left then the right, they are usually going back and forth between fact and creativity to solve a solution.

Questions put you in the driver's seat. The Most Beautiful Woman in the Room really wants someone to see what her real beauty is. Her whole life she has been complimented on her outward appearance. So if you walked up to her and did the same, you will probably get the same old results. Similarly, larger companies that have developed a name for themselves have the same challenge. So many sales people approach them the same way that they begin to all sound the same as well.

The goal should always be "How can one look from the inside out and find that hidden quality that makes this person/company UNIQUE!!!!!!!" The only way to find this is to ask questions that get to the inside.

The Conversation

What is it that you are really looking for? Previously, I told you that you are looking for more opportunity. What does that opportunity look like? What does it sound like? These are interesting questions. The answer is even more interesting. One of the definitions of opportunity is when preparedness meets the right circumstance, however, if you do not know what you are looking or listening for, it really would not matter how prepared you were. Knowing what you want to accomplish or what you are looking for is equally important as knowing how to get there. Let's say for instance that you want to sell 1 million widgets per month to your dream client. It is very unlikely that you can just walk up to this client and ask them to buy 1 million of your widgets per month and they say, SURE! You might have more of a chance of winning the lottery. However, having that goal is not unrealistic. Making that goal happen within the first 5 minutes of a conversation might be. A seasoned sale person realizes that it may take some time to establish the correct foundation so they methodically manage their own expectation by setting smaller goals that lead to the desired outcome. The Most Beautiful Woman in the Room wants to get married and have a very meaningful relationship built on trust and integrity. Believe me, there is not one woman on the face of the earth that would not kill for that. They could have just gotten a divorce with a guy that completely took away their self-respect and if Mr. Right walked up, they would entertain some possibilities. Remember (**Life, sales, the woman All the same!**)   The only thing standing in the way of the million dollar deal or Mr. Right is something called MEMORY! That's it. Let's roll with this for a second. Without memory, we would have no fear. With no fear, there is unlimited OPPORTUNITY! So, I asked a question earlier… what does opportunity look like, or what does it sound like? Opportunity is the place where the person or entity has no hindsight and nothing but foresight. Wow! That means, all you have to do to accomplish anything in your life is to stop looking backward and start looking forward. I had to lay that ground work before I got into the conversation because just like I mentioned earlier, it is important to know where you are going. So please, stop looking in the rearview mirror to drive your car. What you past on the highway of life is already behind you… Now, let's talk about how to get there.

The goal of the conversation is NOT for you talk but rather to listen to what the other person has to say. You will become the ultimate sales person when you say nothing and listen to everything. The Most Beautiful Woman in the Room wants to be heard, so let her talk. I promise you that if you ask the right questions, she will tell you everything you need to impress her. You might not be getting married that night but if you are really listening, you will at least move on to the next level. What is it that you are really listening for?

Opportunity has a certain sound to it.   Sometimes the sound of opportunity is so powerful that you almost have to duck before it knocks you off of your seat. Try to remain poised. The sound of opportunity has many different pitches, however, in my experience it usually starts the same. It usually starts with "HMM…" followed by some gesture of "Tell me more". It is very important to know what it is you are looking or listening for because you may miss it and blow your chances. If you start getting these gestures, then continue with that same train of thought and explore all the possibilities **until you understand why that caught their attention**. It is very important to show you what you are looking for before we get into the actual conversation itself. The questions and conversation would be meaningless unless you have an idea of what it is you are looking for. Opportunity also has a certain look to it as well. I have a deep admiration for professional poker players. I myself do not play the game but, occasionally, I will watch it on television. I am completely amazed when a player receives that one card that is a sure win and they act as if nothing has happened. What a feeling! These individuals have learned how to truly control their emotions. I brought up this example to show you that you may have a winning hand but if you do not understand what you are looking for or what is going to make a winning hand, your work is in vain.

The look of opportunity sometimes starts with a look from the person that you are speaking with that is unique only to opportunity. Watch the person that you are speaking with and if they begin to look up and to the left… they are accessing the creative part of their brain. Better put, they are beginning to look forward. There are many other clues but I am only mentioning one for the sake of being brief. You could easily have someone looking directly at you but be thinking about how to apply your product/service to their challenge.

Discovering what the hidden opportunity with a person could be is like becoming a detective. You have to ask a lot of questions to find what it is. With respect to The Most Beautiful Woman in the Room, it is going to be difficult but not impossible. I have a four stage approach: Compliment, Discovery, Close, and Compliment.

CHAPTER 2 (THE PROCESS)

The Compliment

So the object of all your desires, center of all your dreams, apple of your eye, just walk through the door. WOW! That's all you can say. Immediately you begin thinking about how great it would be to get to know her but... all of a sudden... you begin to remember all the girls you walked up to and got shot down. This deep feeling begins to take control and just like that, you begin to find ways on how NOT to talk to her. You find every little flaw you can find and say "Well, she has a mole on her right hand and I only like moles to be on the left hand." However, as the time passes by, you can't help but to be captivated by her beauty. You want to get to know her and see if she could be your "Mrs. Right.". Somehow you muster up enough courage and stop remembering all the times you got shot down and move your way in her direction. Now you are just a few feet from her and what do you say? We are going to stop right here and talk about the compliment. Every person in the world wants others to notice them. In some form or fashion, there is something that this woman wants the world to see. More than likely, it will be subtle. This is no different from that major firm that you have your eye on to make that million dollar sale to. Remember, you have 90 seconds, that's it, so it might behoove you to say something that they cannot turn down. Try to find the thing that no one else is looking at. Remember, all the other people that have made their approach have crashed landed. I really cannot tell you what to say here. It is different for every person, but I do know that it's something rarely complimented on. The response to your compliment should sound like "Wow, no one has ever noticed that before" or, "That's a new one". Guess what, you just bought yourself another 90 seconds. The compliment is sincere. It is not some line that you heard in a movie, it truly is sincere. The compliment is important because it lets the opposite party know that you are paying attention and are focusing directly on them. It typically creates a natural flow of events that if followed, will lead you naturally to your next destination with ease. It is a type of gift that you can practice all the time to begin to develop proper relationship. Lastly, an honest, well placed compliment may help bring down that wall that most people have surrounding the parameter of their heart. I cannot stress this enough. Please make sure that you are being honest and sincere because if you are not, then you might come off as a used car sales person trying to break down the defenses of the helpless buyer.

Now that you just bought yourself another 90 seconds, what do you do next? Discovery.

Discovery

This part of the sale cycle is extremely important! You could blow the whole deal in less time than it took you to get off the stool and walk over. The goal in the discovery section is to get them to tell you what the opportunity is for yourself. Let me say this in a different way. You have the solution to their problem but you are just looking for the correct way to present it. You could have filet mignon but if you serve it to them on the top of a garbage top then your chances for success is diminished almost to nothing! Secondly, this is not the time for you to talk about yourself. How can you talk and listen at the same time? Remember, this woman has been approached every way in the world so her defenses are at the highest level. This is so similar to the major firm that is called upon hundreds of times per day by sales people trying to get their product sold. Would you buy from one of these people? Probably not! So why are you doing the same thing? **Same actions will produce the same results!**

Discovery is a very indirect way of finding out what their "hot buttons" are without really coming out and asking directly. **The discovery part of the process is a natural flow of the conversation that is led by them, orchestrated by you**. I realize that this may be a bit confusing, however, it would be similar to walking a dog… the dog is leading you but you ultimately are controlling the direction. This is done through a serious of questions. I will tell you that this process takes longer than any other part of the process and you will have to develop a bit of patience. More than half the information that is coming out of the other person's mouth is completely useless. Just plain old "background noise." A popular introduction statement is, "Tell me about yourself". We have to assume that this woman or major firm knows more about themselves than any other topic in the whole world so this cannot be a bad place to start. The worst case scenario is that you bought yourself another 90 seconds (probably a whole lot more). During the time that this woman is talking about herself, you should be listening and thinking at the same time. It is not that hard, if you know what you are looking for. Again, we are listening for OPPORTUNITY. Once that person hits the note of opportunity, simply ask another question that will lead them (and you) in discovering the possibilities of that particular opportunity.

By the way, did I mention earlier that this process was going to take some time? This is good. The value of "time investment" is important because it slowly begins to lock the client in. How many times have you started watching a movie and by the middle of the show you realize that it is awful and will not get any better? However, since you got to the middle, you might as well make it to the end. Well, this is similar to the experiences with people. When talking to The Most Beautiful Woman in the Room, you might find yourself bored by the middle of the conversation, and may realize that this person really is not that beautiful at all. Keep going; never stop until you find what you are looking for. Every single situation is a learning opportunity and the worst thing that could happen is that you made a new friend that may greatly affect your future.

In the discovery part of the conversation, please be keenly aware of patterns. Most of these patterns will show up with commonly used words or gestures. Why is this important? Does it have a meaning? I bring this to light right now because it may lead you to what you are searching for. People are creatures of habit and most people today are condition response. To put this in a better way, if I am driving down the street and a person in the other lane cuts me off without any warning, my natural response is to be upset. If I say, "Wow, you have a wonderful smile" the natural response is to say "Thank you." It is almost too easy. This is why it is very important to look for the patterns in speech or gestures of the person to whom you are speaking with. I am going to go a bit further with this and then bring it home. If people are creatures of habit, then the process of picking a mate and the process of picking a new vendor would be similar, if not exactly the same. The way a person thinks is constant and seldom changes. Only the situations change. This is why in the beginning of the book I suggested that a seasoned sales person should be able to sell any given product/service at any given moment, at any given time, as long as a need is found and your solution makes sense. Why? It is because **SALES IS A PROCESS**! Contrary to popular belief, **GREAT SALES PEOPLE ARE MADE, NOT BORN**! If all these statements are true then you should be able to ask The Most Beautiful Woman in the Room a process question and you should be able to understand how they think. If you understand how they think then you can then present your material in a fashion that would be conducive for how they would buy. Let me give you an example: So you walk up to The Most Beautiful Woman in the Room and strike up a great conversation. She is laughing and everything is going great. She tells you that she is in the process of looking for a new house (by the way, this is a great time for asking a process question). So you ask her "How will you go about making that decision?" She tells you her parameters and says "Well, my budget is X, and I would like to find something that will be close to my job, and I do not want to do a lot of maintenance on the house, and if it had a three car garage it would be great." You ask her why she wants a three car garage and she replies, "Well, I have a lot of junk that I would like to store in the third garage". You may further qualify this conversation by asking some priority questions so you do not have to assume the answer. It will be clear, like … "If you had to choose between the location of your house and how big the garage is, which one would you choose?" The Most Beautiful Woman in the Room is giving a small glimpse to the inside of her mind and how she does things. In the conversation above, she may be giving you the most important down to the least. Most people think this way. The things that they want the most are what they usually state first (this is not always the case but not a bad rule of thumb). The first thing that she says is that she has a budget…so money is important. Next she stated that she wanted to be closer to her job…she may have plans to stay at her job or maybe she hates the traffic in the morning. Another possibility is that she just wants to get more sleep in the morning or save money on gas. This would be a good time for a priority question to gain some clarity on the subject or maybe you log it in your mind for some additional discovery. The next thing that was stated was that she wanted a three car garage. At this particular moment, you have an outline of the process but you do not have enough information to make a good assessment of really why she thinks the way that she does. The outline itself creates more questions. This process lends to itself. The more you follow the process, the more specific and detailed the questions become until finally you look up and you have spent an hour talking about HER and not YOU. You were buying 90 seconds at a time the entire way by asking her questions. If we can now apply this exact same process to that magical client, then you are half way there. Why … **Life, Sales, The Woman…all the same thing!**

In the discovery section we have talked a lot about questions and how to get the object of your desire to open up to you. One of the most important things to remember at all times is "If you do not know where you are going, then any road will seem like the right way to go". This statement can be applied to your life as well. Life is a balance of consistency and chaos happening at the same time. Individuals that are methodical and deliberate have a hard time with the spontaneous things that occur every day. They feel that if they are not in control then they are out of control causing stress as a result. Conversely, individuals who live life on the edge and are drawn to the flow of life have difficulty with structured events and planned outcomes, again, causing stress. In this next section we will dive into this and find out who you are. Your greatest strength is also the very thing that will cause you the most pain if not properly managed.

The Close

The close is the most natural part of the selling process and the most important to you! To close any deal means that you are being rewarded for following the correct instructions and your payment comes in the currency of money. So many sales people, old and new, still ask the same question…How do you close? If a sales person methodically goes through the correct process of selling anything then the buyer will be asking you "Where do I sign?" However, this still does not answer the question on how to close. The most important thing in closing any deal is to solve the pain. It could be perceived pain or a real corporate pain. I am going to take a moment here and tell you a brief story. One of my first real jobs out of college was working for a well-known copier company. To this day, I credit my thirst and zeal for selling to this company. I had a sales manager who really rode me to learn everything I could about every part of the sales cycle. I give him the credit of bringing out of me what I refused to bring out myself. His name was David and he made me read at least 20 books and attend half a dozen seminars and training programs known to man at that time. At one of these seminars I bought a cassette tape (this is showing you how old I am) on closing. I listened to this tape every day. I listened to this tape on the way to work and on the way back home. I wore the tape out until one day it just did not work anymore. On this tape, there were 23 closing techniques that the person on this tape not only provided the name of the closing technique, but also used it in context. IT WAS GREAT!!! I listened to that tape for about 14 months until I could use every single close without even thinking about it. However, the problem was that it just did not seem to work in real life the way the guy on the tape made it sound. It made my clients feel like they were BEING SOLD!!! I became a shark and everyone else around me were tuna. Let me tell you, tuna are real fast. Although I did real well, you cannot treat your prospects like a piece of meat! I brought this up because even though you may have all these cool techniques for getting someone to say yes, it is way better when they ask you, "Where do I sign?" Well since then, we now have the internet and there is not too much information that cannot be found. What this means to all sales people is that your customer may be more educated about whatever it is you are selling than you are. The hunter easily can become the hunted. How do you get past that??? Here we go!

The secret to closing is to lead the customer into a situation where they come up with the answer to their own challenge! That's it!!! To put this another way, your job is to get them to creatively think about the challenge and then to solve the challenge that they presented with logical facts that your product or service offers. Let's bring this back home to the most beautiful woman in the room.

So, you have gotten enough nerve to start the conversation with this individual. You started off with the compliment and you are asking all the right questions, but do you remember why you are asking all these question? To buy yourself another 90 seconds of opportunity. In the beginning of this book, I told you that you must know where you are going before you know how to get there. This is the key to closing. As you are asking this woman questions, you start heading down the path that you want to take, which is that you would like to go on a date with her. More importantly, you want HER to want to go out on a date with you! Somehow in your conversation you must find out what is keeping her from doing just that. So you may ask, "So…how long have you been single?" Her response may be, "well 10 years, one year, or I just broke up with my boyfriend"… the point here is that there may be an infinite amount of possible answers. The only thing that you should hear is that "Yes I am available". This is no different than when you are sitting in front of a decision maker at a major firm and you may ask "How long have you been without …" and their response will be "Oh... 10years, one year, or we just parted ways with our last vendor". The only thing that you really just heard is "YES I AM AVAILABLE". This is opportunity right in your face. You know for a fact that if you just present your material in the right way then you may have a chance to win. Your next question is one of the most important questions that you could ever ask. It is a bit corny but it works. The next question is a "How does that make you feel" question. Asking this question will expose the fear, no matter how it is answered. It also will tell you a lot about the person that you are dealing with. Remember, normal sales people are talking about their product or service, the seasoned sales person is listening for the opportunity to solve the challenge. Ok, let's continue with The Most Beautiful Woman in the Room. So you ask, "How does that make you feel?" DO NOT LEAD HER TO AN ANSWER!!!! You want her to tell you the truth, no matter what the answer is. It could be, "I feel great being single. It's the best thing that has ever happened to me", or "well, not very good. I really miss having a significant other to share my life with". Similarly, the question may be asked to the major firm like "How do you feel or how has that effected your business?" and the response may be "Wow, it was one of the best moves that we ever did", or "Well, business is not the same without that product or service that they were providing" Either answer works for the seasoned sales person. A good sales person simply follows the path that has the most pain and then solves the pain with their product or service. The way to solve the pain is not by a direct statement but rather it is a question that again gets the person to think about the new possible outcome. The question is presented right after the pain has been discovered. You should use "if, then" statements to present the new alternative. An example of this would be "if I was able to …then how would that effect your bottom line?" Let's move the question to The Most Beautiful Woman in the Room because it may be easier to see. Let's say that the woman has just told you in the discovery part of your conversation that she is lonely because her dog that she has had for the past 13 years just died. At this point you might assume that buying a new pet would be the answer, however, you really do not have enough substantial information to determine this. A trial close or pre-close might be your best bet in this situation to test the water a bit and see if this would be a viable solution. "Well… what if there was a way to get you the same kind of dog, with all the same qualities as your last pet? Would you then still be unhappy?" These types of questions are commitment questions. They are either yes or no. If the answer is yes, then you can easily plot your course and move forward. However, if the answer is no, then you might ask, ""what would?" Again, this would elicit more conversation to narrow down what the solution is. By the way, this requires absolutely no thought from you because you are just waiting on the answer that **they are giving to you**. At the end of the conversation, if you have been an excellent listener and have taken great notes, just repeat the trial close question with the new information and wait for them to say yes. It's like the art of selling without selling!!!!!

The Compliment (2)

This may sound a bit redundant; however, this shows the object of your desires that you were really paying attention. You are complimenting them on their new fantastic discovery. I often like to use the word "Wow". Wow to me is a very positive word. It is a word of expression that shows surprise as well as admiration. You must pull this off as if it really were a surprise. Pretty hard to do if you knew the answer to the question before you got started. In a lot of ways The Most Beautiful Woman in the Room is fragile and needs to be stroked just a bit. She needs to be reassured that she made the correct decision. Even if they come off like they are affected by nothing, believe me, she loves every minute someone is paying real attention to what she has to say and not at just how she looks. You know you did the ending compliment right if she responds like "I am happy I had you here to help me" or "you really think so?" Both responses are acceptable because one denotes a sense of confidence in your cooperation with her and the other is confidence that you can perform the way that you say you can. Equally, the corporation will respond the same way. Their response sounds something like this "well... thank you very much...

we try to… (Monologue)" or "well, we really hope that you can perform on that solution, we have been looking for that for some time now". Same response, different application. By the way, the ending compliment really removes most barriers with respect to trust. You are putting them at ease by indirectly letting them know that you are on their side and are completely interested in solving the challenge at hand.

CHAPTER 3

QUESTIONS…QUESTIONS…QUESTIONS

Questions are the most important weapon in the arsenal of a sales person. You might be asking "What questions do I ask?" That in itself is a great question. All of your questions should be geared toward finding the pain. That is it. There are only 5 items in life that The Most Beautiful Woman in the Room will ever ask you... they are the following (not in order):

How reliable are you?
How dependable are you?
How much do you cost?
How much service is provided with you?
Are you easy to use?

I know this sounds funny but it is very true. By the way, as you guessed, every corporation is also asking the same questions. Of course, the solution to your life challenges are all wrapped up into these categories. Why you may ask? Remember (**Life, Sales, The Woman… all the same thing**) Interestingly, you may be surprised that price may not be at the top of the list. That is why it is extremely imperative to listen to what is truly important to the client, not to what you think is important. Let's go over each one.

How reliable are you?

Reliability has some very subtle meanings… The most obvious is something that is going to be around for a long time. The undertone meaning is accuracy, honesty and integrity. The Most Beautiful Woman in the Room is looking for someone who is accurate, honest and has the utmost integrity in their dealings. They are constantly flattered by meaningless compliments as well as overzealous promises. A huge mistake with sales people that are just beginning their sales careers is that they OVER PROMISE AND UNDER DELIVER. We all have done it. We all have gotten caught up in the moment, just happy that we are being entertained by the object of our desire and then a question comes up that we really do not have the answer to….BAM!!! Before we can even police it, the words… "YES I CAN DO THAT" fly right out of our mouths!!!! The sales person with a bit more maturity knows to either defer that question until it can be accurately answered and/or TELL THE TRUTH. **The ugly truth is more important than a beautiful lie**. The absolute worst thing that will happen is that you will gain respect from your client. I have gotten more return phone calls from companies that I flat out told the truth to and said that our firm cannot do what was requested.

Reliability will be asked to you in a number of different ways. "How long has your company been in business?" or "How often do you have to repair your…?" The Most Beautiful Woman in the Room may phrase it like this, "So… How long have you been doing what you do?" Reliability question. Same question, different application. Reliability questions usually start off with the word *How*.

How dependable are you?

Most people will say that dependability and reliability are the same. I will say that they both can be used interchangeably. However, I view dependability to mean a right now situation or scenario, short term or immediate. I hear the word used a lot when people want something right at the moment. Also, the undertone meaning of dependability is consistence of performance on demand. I will do my best to put this together. Dependability is how often you can perform under immediate pressure. The Most Beautiful Woman in the Room wants to know this. Most beautiful things in life require a bit more maintenance. This would stand to reason. An example of this would be a rose and a weed. A rose would be considered by most to be a beautiful flower. It may take a bit more maintenance to grow. On the other hand, a weed pretty much grows in every scenario. Hell, you have to work real hard to get it not to grow. The Most Beautiful Woman in the Room wants to know if she can depend on you to take care of her needs. That means under pressure as well as no pressure involved. This is no different from the corporate company that you have your eye on. The question will come up if you can take care of their consistent needs. The question that will be asked to you will sound something like this, "Will your product be able to handle…?" The Most Beautiful Woman in the Room will ask it something like this "So…how often do you…?" Same question, different application. Dependable questions often start out with the words *"How" or "Can"*.

How much do you cost?

"That which must be GIVEN, DONE or UNDERTAKEN in order to obtain a thing". This is dictionary.com's definition of price. This is my favorite question. I love to be asked how much the price is of something. It is the question that we have all feared at one point in our sales careers. Price is my favorite question because it is the easiest to conquer. How much something is, is completely relative to the value of the product or service being offered or provided. Most people will be surprised that the more beautiful something is, the less likely it is that price will be a concern.

The Most Beautiful Woman in the Room will gladly pay the price for that which she perceives as valuable to her. If service has been a challenge for the corporate giant that you have your eye on then they will gladly pay a bit extra for solving the problem. The key to selling price is PERCEIVED VALUE. Price should never come up in the beginning of a conversation. If you walk into a room full of executives and the first question they ask you is "How much does it cost?"…you have to find a way to not answer that question and get them talking about themselves in a hurry. I have found that one of the best ways to do that is by saying this: "Well that is a good question. By the way, before I answer that question, how in the world did you out revenue your competition 2 to1 last quarter?" or "I am glad that you asked me that, unfortunately, that really depends on our conversation here today. I need a bit more information to make sure that I give you an accurate number". Here is another one… "I am really here more on a fact finding conversation to see if your company will really need these services. There may be a way that I could solve your problem without any out of pocket cost to you!" Whew!!!! Just bought myself another 90 seconds. Similarly, The Most Beautiful Woman in the Room is thinking the same thing. She says this to herself all the time and sooner or later she will ask herself--- "How much is it going to cost me if I get myself involved with you?" The only way to get price out of the way is to have a possible solution to solve the pain before you get to that conversation. We will talk more about solving the pain in the next section. Price questions normally start off with *How* but occasionally begin with *What*.

How much service is provided with you?

Serviceability.

Remember the definition of price explained above. It said "that which must be given, done, or undergone in order to obtain a thing." If this is the definition of price, then service would be on the other side of the equal sign in the mathematical equation. Service is completely undervalued to a small firm but for a large corporation, service is one of the key decision making points. It has occurred to me that **the more valuable you are, the more service is important to you**. The lack of great service could cost a major corporation million or even billions. Wow!!! There are over 37 different definition of the word service in the dictionary. The Most Beautiful Woman in the Room wants to be SERVICED!!! The question is, how?! Every corporation and woman is different; however, they all want the same thing. Usually, this is the part of your conversation that will take the longest. It requires total bi-directional honest communication. Great service is one of the keys to success in closing The Most Beautiful Woman in the Room and a corporation alike.

Are you easy to use?

Ease of use can be a huge stumbling block in a sale. You can have the best product, an acceptable price, with great service; however, if it is too hard to use or integrate inside the structure, it will be an act of God to close this deal. One of the hardest challenges for people is to think creatively on their feet. Most people have been trained or cultivated to become good students or to follow a certain set of rules that typically do not require us to use much of our creative mind. Our society today, sadly, has become one that is conditioned and response whereby little to no thinking is required. Everything is automatic. Creative thinking is a must to becoming an expert sales person. You do not have to know everything about everything to be successful. You just need to know where everything could possibly fit. The Most Beautiful Woman in the Room would love to be swept off of her feet by Prince Charming who has all of the qualities that she is looking for. Be that as it may, if Prince Charming cannot find a way to easily and successfully integrate his life into hers, chances are he will be hearing… "Houston, we have a problem!"

CHAPTER 4

Personal Discovery

We have been talking a lot about situations that are outside of ourselves. I would like to take a moment to really dive inside and discover who you are and where you are really going. The great things about this statement is, once you understand yourself, a natural sense of confidence will begin to arise simply because you will understand your strengths and liabilities. More importantly, you will begin to know how to apply them which would allow you the most success.

 In the past, I searched for the one answer that would completely change my life into perfect harmony. I have asked personal friends and even people who I have just met what it is that makes me, me. I was looking for the positive things that people would say that I am. I got a lot of surprising answers to my questions. I found out that what I think I am on the inside may not be what I am projecting on the outside. I spent so much time working on the inside that I forgot about the outside. This caused me to think about BALANCE. Only now do I understand this and how important it is to life. Whoever came up with the saying of "opposites attract" completely knew what they were talking about. People attract the opposite of themselves to create a balance within their lives. If a structured, controlling individual attracted another individual of like mind, then there would be no room for this thing called CHAOS. Without chaos, there would be no stress. Without stress there would be no reason to stop and take a look at yourself. If you never took a look at yourself then there would be no reason to CHANGE. If there is no reason to change then there would not be any reason to GROW. If you never grew, then there would be no reason to LEARN. If there is no reason to learn, then there is no reason to LIVE! Life is a journey of secrets. The secret to your journey often lies in the chaos that it created to get your attention. Now that this has been said, I think it is extremely important that we look at this opposite because sometimes in order to be found, you must first be lost.

If you really want to change your life, then you must entertain that which you fear most. Most people, whether they want to admit it or not, are afraid of rejection. For some reason, we all take it personal. The Most Beautiful Woman in the Room represents something we want desperately but believe we do not deserve. That is why she is the object of our desire. Similarly, the major firm is also a representation of that exact same fear. Think about it. If we could truly picture ourselves with this beautiful woman or major firm, dream house, fancy and expensive car, etc…and we truly believe that we deserve this, then we would no longer fear it. As a matter of fact, it would be part of our everyday experience that would bring consistent joy and pleasure. So your fear is really keeping you away from being happy! Most people would even defend it violently simply because that's the way they grew up or that's what they were taught when they were young! What is really interesting about this is that we would naturally move on to the next item that we feared, looking at it as if IT were The Most beautiful Woman in the Room. You would do this because it is just outside of your mental reach, therefore, it becomes what you desire. It would take us a life time to conquer all that fear. This means that if we do not take the time to identify what our fears are, face it, and conquer it, then we are not growing at all. Most people go through life on auto pilot. Condition response is what it is called. For every scenario, there is an automatic response. For this reason, we never use our mind to actively think about the outcome. Studies show that the average human uses less than 10% of the total capacity of their brain. What a waste. If we only used 10% of the capacity of an average car, would we even know that it could take us places? We might even think that the car was nothing more than an oversized couch. I brought this up because without knowing what it is that we are dealing with, then we will never know how to be victorious over what it is that is keeping us from being truly successful at whatever it is we really want. Biblical teaching states very clearly that in order to be successful that we must FIRST believe in something that does not exist. Plainly put, we must first visualize ourselves already victorious. To sum this up… once you have The Most Beautiful Woman in the Room in your mind, she no longer is something to be feared but something to be respected. Remember, the eye of the stove produces fire that if not respected, can burn or kill. Conversely, if it is respected, it can cook a good meal for life. That feeling of fear somehow turns into respect. Now your actions will produce the physical equivalent of your constant mental focus. Once there is nothing left to fear from her, you are already successful. Everything that has been stated first starts with your mental visualization of that process.

Walking through the door together

I realize that this is a strange title. As strange as it is, no one wants to be alone so it seems to fit The Most Beautiful Woman in the room has now given you the time of day. You started off the conversation with the compliment to get her attention. You followed up the compliment with a discovery conversation to find out more about her inner beauty and pain. You lead her to her own solution with "if, then" questions and you also complimented her on how smart she was with coming up with the right solution. Now, what do you do next? This is where you must be willing to commit. This is a scary word for most guys. Remember, you already have The Most Beautiful Woman in the Room. All you have to do now is keep her. With the major firm at your feet now, you must hold their hand and walk them through this new process. You must become reliable, dependable, give great service, at the right price, and make it easy for them to do business with you. You must walk through the door together. So many sales people at this point will leave this up to someone else to take care of their client. This is one of the biggest mistakes you can ever make. This one client will feed you and your family for life if it is handled right. This is no different from making that special connection with The Most Beautiful Woman in the Room. Would you leave this woman to be taken care of with your old frat buddies from college? Of course not! You already know the outcome of that! Commitment is so important. This is not a game. Live your life with integrity, honesty, and be truthful to yourself. It will pay huge dividends to you and your next generation. You have worked so hard to have this opportunity. Do not blow it by slacking off because this is where the real work begins. The most important thing that I want you to remember is this…**YOUR POTENTIAL HAS AN 1:2 RATIO WITH YOUR COMMITMENT!**

Let me say this another way, if you are ½ married… you are going to be fully divorced! (Get the picture?)

Do nothing for free

I went through the early part of my life just giving away the gifts that I had received. Consequently, I always found that I was a bit poor in some respect of my life. It might have been financially, spiritually, physically, socially, or mentally but somehow my statue was diminished in some respect. What makes this more interesting is that all of the individuals I gave my information to became successful in the areas that I gave. This is almost a paradox with what most people actually believe. I profess to be a Christian but the Bible talks more about balance than it does just giving. We are taught that it is all about giving, giving, giving, however, we rarely focus on the verses that deal with receiving. One verse about this subject which makes this very clear is Matthew 7:6, *"Do not give what is holy to dogs, and do not throw your pearls before swine…"* If you want to know what happens when you do, then read the rest for yourself. You may figure out what you have been doing wrong. When I say never do anything for free, I want to qualify what I am saying. There should be something that you are receiving that will edify your life in some form or fashion. If this is not the case, then there is a parasitic relationship that is going on, sometimes without you even being aware of it. Life is about mutually beneficial relationships that create a synergy between or among the parties that are involved. This is true in all relationships both business and personal. To relate this to The Most Beautiful Woman in the Room, if you come baring gifts and she is just taking them, what are you receiving? Conversely, how have you really helped her? Free has no value. Stop paying for everything. I know sales people who cater lunch just so people can listen to what they are selling. 9 times out of 10, no one in the room even heard what you had to say. They are there for the free meal. Create a win-win situation where both parties are both giving and receiving at the same time.

At the end of the day!

Great sales people are MADE not BORN! That's right, I said it! Every person that has the normal faculties of life can be an exceptional sales person. There is nothing out of your reach, including The Most Beautiful Woman in the Room. In my humble but convicted point of you, if individuals would stop looking at what they do not have and start concentrating on what they do possess, that is 50% of the battle. The most beautiful woman is already yours… your job is not to lose her. By following a very simple process of just keeping her talking about what she knows best (which is herself) you have put yourself head and shoulders above 90% of the average sales people who think they have a chance. Moreover, truly listening to what is important to her will put you way ahead of the game. In addition, if you can also find out her way of making decisions then you have done your job as a professional. The only way that you will not make this sale is if they truly do not have the means to buy your product or service.

I would like to conclude this writing with "you are your greatest asset as well as your greatest liability." Life is truly about perspective. Your perspective on life is determined by your beliefs. Your beliefs have been molded and shaped by basically what you have decided to be true. Which could mean that some things that you believe to be true, may not be true (I hope you are getting this). The only way to begin living the life you were intended to live is to take some inventory of what gifts you ACTUALLY have, not the ones you think you have. I am going to make this simple for you and put this in a step by step form…

1. Write down on a piece of paper all of your gifts.
2. Write down your dreams, goals, and aspirations.
3. Look at your gifts and write down the correct course of action to take that will lead you to your dreams, using your gifts.

   Let me put that another way. What is the correct response to your abilities? (I hope you got it).

   Let me say it again and make it plain. What is your response-ability?

Your perspective on life will determine your destiny. Let no one tell you who you are and what you can or cannot do. There is nothing, absolutely NOTHING you cannot do or accomplish once you have the correct information. The Most Beautiful Woman in the Room is waiting for you.

www.ingramcontent.com/pod-product-compliance
Lightning Source LLC
Chambersburg PA
CBHW021047180526
45163CB00005B/2324